All Of Us Are Going To Die, But Not All Of Us Are Going To Enjoy Eternity

THE PRESENT
into
THE RAPTURE
into
TRIBULATION
into
THE 1000 YEAR KINGDOM
into
ETERNITY

By
Biblical Non-Scholar
Mel Stuckey

A narrative on eternity from studying The Bible, Biblical Web Sites
nd Stephen Armstrong's Verse by Verse Ministries' REVELATION Series

THE

REVELATION

COMMENTARY

It's my prayer that nothing in this narrative contradicts, nor adds to nor takes away from God's Holy Word.

For the full story read the Bible.

Clay Bridges
P R E S S

ISBN: 978-1-68488-082-9 (Hardback)
ISBN: 978-1-68488-081-2 (Paperback)
eISBN: 978-1-68488-083-6

Special Sales: Most Clay Bridges titles are available in special quantity discounts. Custom imprinting or excerpting can also be done to fit special needs. Contact Clay Bridges at Info@ClayBridgesPress.com

CONTENTS

THE PRESENT

THE PRESENT

IN BRIEF: Current times where most of us are consumed with everyday living.

Our very existence is one partly of flesh and partly of spirit (spirit and soul are the same). The flesh of our bodies is destined to return to dust at our physical death, but our spirit lives on eternally. When our physical body dies, our spirit must immediately go to some new place.

Our spirit is always conscious, never asleep, destined to exist along with a complimentary physical body. Everyone's spirit is continually restless until peace in God is found.

Believers are those fortunate enough to have come to faith in Christ (believers and Saints are the same). Saints do include Jewish and Gentile believers.

Faith is an expression of hope because it accepts something as true before it can be seen. Once something can be seen, accepting the truth of it no longer requires faith…it's become self-evident.

All of us have eternal spirits that coexist with our sinful, temporary physical bodies. Believers' spirits are destined to eventually be linked with splendid, eternal, and sinless physical bodies. This God initiated act, where new, everlasting bodies are fused together with our current souls, is called resurrection!

After death, each person's spirit will continue to exist in full consciousness yet without a body until a future day of resurrection, when God joins our spirit with a newly appointed, eternally permanent body.

Each person's spirit at death will experience a dramatically different destiny depending on whether, while living, the person was a believer … or a non-believer … and depending on when they live in history.

Revelation, the final book of the Bible, describes alternate pathways which can be taken through eternity. Believers' final destination is eternally rewarding. Unbelievers' final destination is eternally unpleasant, because they will experience being eternally separated from the presence of God.

Location of things is important, so let's review six biblically important vaults or unique sites. There's the earth's surface, where we all live and die today, and our Lord's domain in Heaven above (when our spirits reach Heaven is covered a few pages later), plus three underground, intermediate, after-death, temporary, spirits' locations.

> (a) There's Abraham's Bosom where the souls of Old Testament believers (OT Saints) who are saved, have rested in comfort until Christ and angels escorted them to Heaven. The souls of OT Saints could not go directly to Heaven at the moment of their death, because the atonement of Christ had yet to be made on the cross.

> (b) There's Hades (Hell / Gehenna) where the souls of all who have died without faith in God's promises (unbelievers) temporarily reside, in a dreadful environment.

> (c) There's the gruesome Abyss where the Devil and all his demons will reside temporarily when God sends them there.

These underground destinations are distinct, separate holding centers.

In addition to these five above destinations, there is a permanent, everlasting, place of torment, and eternal damnation called the Lake of Fire. This Lake of Fire exists in the Heavenly places outside our sight but in the presence of the angels.

We now live in an age biblically identified as the Church Age. It started over 2000 years ago with a God initiated event called the Pentecost (a world altering descent of the Holy Spirit upon the Apostles and other followers of Jesus Christ while they were in Jerusalem celebrating the Feast of Weeks).

In Pentecost, through today, all of us have lived in this Church Age, where God's saving grace turned from Israel, his chosen people, and was directed toward enlightening and saving Gentiles.

To keep similar appearing words and terms clear as we move forward, Church Age represents a time period: Church is shorthand for Church Age believers as a group: Saints is another name for believers: Church Age Saints are also called Christ's Bride.

Scripture makes a distinction between Jews of Israel and the Church. There is some overlap because, individually, many Jews believe in Jesus as their Messiah and are therefore part of the Church.

The current Church Age comes to an end at the Rapture.

The spirits of all Church Age Saints join Christ in Heaven at the moment of their death.

THE RAPTURE
FOLLOWS...

THE RAPTURE

THE RAPTURE

IN BRIEF: The Rapture is the future moment when Christ, in a twinkling of an eye, appears in the clouds, draws up with Him believers from the earth, and resurrects all Church Saints' bodies to fit them for eternity.

Defining "resurrect" can be elusive. In this narrative we mean resurrect/resurrected/resurrection as God's joining of a person's old eternal spirit with their new eternal body. All of us, whether believers or nonbelievers, will eventually enter eternity resurrected (our old eternal spirit joined with our new eternal body.) Believers will enjoy eternity with God. Unbelievers won't.

The Rapture will inaugurate a period that the Bible characterizes as the "great day of His wrath." This will be a time of unprecedented difficulty which will affect Israel and all nations. The purpose will be to prepare Israel for her Messiah.

An understanding of the Rapture is "essential information for the soul". It's one of the world's most paramount coming events.

At the Rapture, separate pathways into the future for believers and for non-believers are made unmistakably clear.

The Rapture of the Church occurs prior to the Tribulation. Its purpose is for Christ to graciously remove all Saints prior to returning His attention to the sins of Israel and her disobedience under the Old Covenant.

> The Old Covenant was a mutual agreement God made with the Israeli Nation as they were entering into the Promised Land that God was giving them. Noncompliance penalties were clear and severe.
>
> The main purpose of this Old Covenant was to point all Israelites to the coming Christ, that the nation could be justified by faith.
>
> Before even making it to the Promised Land, Israel resisted God's authority. After entering the Promised Land, rebellion and unfaithfulness was the norm over the next seven centuries. It became so blatant that Israel effectively abandoned this marriage-like mutual commitment.

The Rapture is an all-important end times event where Jesus Christ returns for His Church Saints. It's a time of both resurrection and judgement (judgement in this case referring to assignment of earned rewards to Saints).

At the time of the Rapture, Church believers who have died, along with believers who are still living, will experience an instantaneous transformation to fit them for eternity.

Believers will meet the Lord in the air. This will all occur in a moment.

In short, the Rapture is the return of Christ in the clouds to remove all believers from the earth before the time of God's wrath (the following seven years of Tribulation).

The Rapture is sometimes incorrectly associated with the Second Coming of Christ, the event when Jesus again sets foot on earth, returns to combat evil, and establishes His Millennial Kingdom. While the Rapture and the Second Coming of Christ have similarities, they are separate events occurring at separate times.

The Rapture is a time of resurrection - *when Church Saints receive new, imperishable and sin free bodies.* But OT Saints are not resurrected (given new eternal bodies) when Church Saints are resurrected.

This divergence can seem confusing, in that all Saints are not resurrected at the same time.

Church Age Saints' Resurrection:

As Church Age Saints encounter death and are laid to rest, their eternal spirits join Jesus immediately in the Heavenly Throne Room (with Christ in Heaven).

They receive their resurrected bodies at the moment of the Rapture.

OT Saints' Resurrection:

In the time before Christ's first coming, Jews were saved by faith in God's word that He would bring Israel a Messiah. Today a Jew is saved by faith in God's word that He did bring a Messiah, and the Messiah is Jesus. Apart from this faith no Jew is saved.

After Christ's crucifixion, He descended into the earth following His death. There He spoke to the OT Saints waiting in Abraham's Bosom. Jesus introduced Himself as the Messiah these Saints had anticipated in faith and explained the Lord's plan of salvation.
At the conclusion of three days' time, Jesus ascended into Heaven, and the OT Saints were escorted directly into Heaven. Abraham's Bosom thus emptied.

Tribulation's martyred "two witnesses" (two OT Saints whom God calls to be His witnesses during Tribulation), are resurrected during the Tribulation... followed by Abraham's Bosom OT Saints - who receive their new eternal bodies at Christ Second Coming, following Tribulation.

Thus, OT Saints do not at the Rapture receive their new everlasting bodies. They do receive their new imperishable bodies at Christ's Second Coming, following Tribulation.

Some are surprised by the thought that the OT Saints will not be resurrected until the end of the Tribulation. But the Rapture is a promise to the Church, and the Church only.

Tribulation Saints' Resurrection:
Those who enter the Tribulation as non-believers, but who repent and become believers during this terrible seven-year period are called Tribulation Saints or Tribulation Martyrs. These Saints receive their new imperishable bodies at Christ's Second Coming, following Tribulation.

Millennial Saint's Resurrection:

Those believers alive at the end of Tribulation will enter the 1000 Year Kingdom Period (Millennial Kingdom) in normal bodies, and will be resurrected at the end of this age when Christ judges all believers and non-believers.

So, the resurrection of the righteous, occurs in stages, beginning with Christ, continuing with the Church at the Rapture, then with Tribulation and OT Saints at Christ's Second Coming, culminating with resurrection of Millennial born believers at the end of this age when Christ judges all believers and non-believers.

The Rapture is also a time of judgement - for Church Saints after they've received their new eternal, imperishable bodies.

This is not a judgment to determine their salvation but for rewards for their earthly labor on Christ's behalf.

Christ's rewards are for believers' blessed deeds while on earth that earn opportunity for greater responsibility for serving in Christ's future everlasting government. They are our inheritance in His kingdom. Only the saved (believers) can earn Heavenly rewards because the Lord does not offer salvation based on works. Faith alone is our means to Heaven.

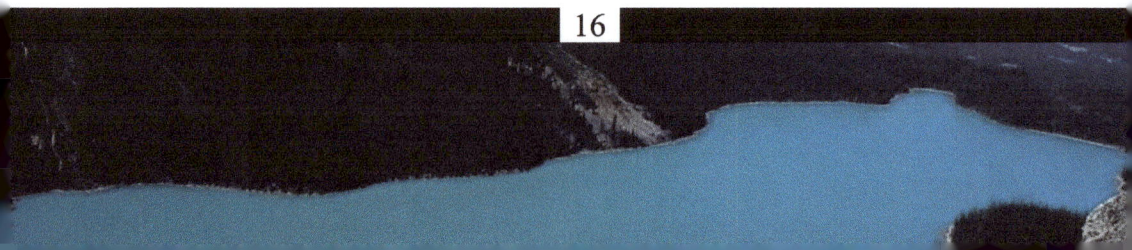

TRIBULATION FOLLOWS

TRIBULATION

TRIBULATION

IN BRIEF: The Tribulation is the future, seven-year time period that only unbelievers will enter into, when God will wreak havoc on the universe and finish His discipline of Israel.

We reach the end of the Church Age after the Rapture. No believers now remain on earth because they have all been "Raptured" and their spirits are in Heaven.

Then begins the seven-years of the Tribulation, a time of unprecedented suffering. Its end to be marked by the War of Armageddon.

This Tribulation period is necessary because of the agreement God made with Israel (thousands of years ago) in the Mosaic (Moses) Covenant. The Mosaic covenant set a standard for God's relationship with His people - that is still in effect.

In this Covenant, the Lord told Israel that unless the "entire nation" kept His law perfect for all generations, they would suffer severe consequences. Only when they "as an entire nation" call out for Him, will He return to them as promised.

Jesus set the terms for His Second Coming for His people...they must call out for Him as their Messiah!

When they call out for Him, then He will return to them on earth as promised! The trials of Tribulation will create the circumstances under which the nation of Israel will experience that change of heart.

The seven years of Tribulation is split into two, 3 ½ year periods in which there will be a series of unimaginable cataclysmic upheavals of nature and the universe.

Those who become believers during Tribulation will be targets for persecution – even to death. The martyrdom of those who become believers will be concentrated in the second half of Tribulation.

First Half of Tribulation

During the first 3 ½ years of Tribulation, while the Antichrist (discussed later) is rising in earthly power, the Lord is still at work bringing to faith a new generation of believers on an increasingly desolate earth.

Despite all of the God initiated calamities taking place, the Temple continues to be open, and the Jewish people worship there.

Two God-sent witnesses wearing sackcloth will prophesy during this first half of Tribulation. These men will perform much like the Old Testament prophets. They have the power to shut up the sky from sending rain, turn water into blood, and strike the earth with plagues.

They will be blamed for everything bad that happens. As these prophets finish their testimony after 3 ½ years, the Lord will allow them to be killed by the Antichrist and their bodies will lie in the streets of Jerusalem for 3 ½ days. Then the Lord will miraculously resurrect their dead bodies so that they return to life for all to see. And as their enemies watch in wonder, these men are taken to Heaven in their resurrected bodies.

During this time, the Lord also brings 144,000 Jewish men to faith so that they will serve Him in proclaiming the Gospel, and they in turn produce many new believers from all over the world.

At the mid-point of Tribulation, the Lord makes a series of dramatic moves to prepare the earth for the next 3 ½ years. Among those dramatic moves is the establishment of a place of protection for all those believing Jews on earth which includes the 144,000 Jewish men. This place of protection, Petra (or Botzrah), will become a fortress in the desert for the second half of Tribulation. The Lord supernaturally protects this remnant for 3 ½ years in Petra preventing the Devil from wiping out believing Israel.

Petra is a natural rock fortress located about 150 miles south of both Jerusalem and Amman, Jordan, about midway between Damascus, Syria, and the Red Sea.

Second Half of the Tribulation

As the Tribulation reaches the 3 ½ year mid-point the earth lies devastated. About ½ of the earth's population has died, about ⅓ of the earth is inhabitable, and over ⅓ of all water becomes undrinkable. It's become a tough place just to exist.

A ten-king, political chain of command emerges that now rules the inhabited earth. Soon these ten are reduced to a seven-king ruling body. And all the while, a charismatic man, the Antichrist, is gaining worldwide attention as a political and military leader.

God permits Satan to indwell the body of this charismatic man and through this union the Antichrist becomes the sole world leader and object of the world's attention and worship. The seven kings report to Him and are also under the control of Satan, who has declared war against all Jews and believing Gentiles.

Claiming to be God, the Antichrist desecrates the Tribulation Temple, seats himself in the mercy seat, and puts an end to other worship.

Another evil man gains notoriety and becomes spokesman for the Antichrist. He's called the False Prophet… a zealot who by the power of Satan is permitted to perform miraculous signs. This False Prophet enforces the decree to worship the Antichrist through economic and numerous other means:

- Every citizen on earth must take a mark on the right hand or the forehead in order to buy or sell anything. Those who take the mark will be protected from government's wrath and will be allowed to buy and sell, but those who refuse the mark will be killed.
- So individuals can become believers, in which case they will be persecuted, and probably will die.
- Or they can worship the Antichrist, in which case they are no longer eligible to become a believer.

In essence, Satan tries to create a false trinity to mirror the real trinity:

- The Christ is imitated by the Antichrist
- The Holy Spirit is imitated by the False Prophet
- The unseeable Father is imitated by Satan

War of Armageddon - Ending The Tribulation

Babylon is the seat of power for the Antichrist during the time of Tribulation. And as Babylon is the symbol for Satan and evil, so Jerusalem symbolizes the opposite. It's the City of God and a place of redemption.

The Lord has narrowed the focus of the world on to these two locations.

The Satan controlled Antichrist gathers Gentile military forces in preparation for a battle against God and God's people… the War of Armageddon, which is carried out in not one, but a series of stages.

The Devil's aim is to eliminate any final resistance to the Antichrist's reign and in the process, prevent Christ's promised return.

The Antichrist's army lays siege to Jerusalem. Outnumbered Jewish inhabitants cower, fully expecting to be massacred.

Two parts to Jerusalem are cut off by the enemy and defeated. These two parts are the sections of Israel in the north and south, where all Jews living there will be killed without mercy.

Only the remaining, barricaded Jews in the middle third of Jerusalem remain alive. Desperation is rampant! These Jews are being put through a life-threatening trial to refine them.

Then giving in to God's pouring out of the Holy Spirit, all these surviving Jews make a "national confession of faith" that Jesus is the Messiah. Their repentance will be honest and true and wholehearted. They now (finally) as a nation put faith in Jesus as their Messiah.

In the moment the "entire Jewish Nation" confesses Christ, He will answer their plea and descend to the earth a second time, accompanied by the Church saints and an army of angels. He comes to earth this second time as the all-powerful warrior of judgement.

Christ's arrival on earth is at Petra. He then approaches Jerusalem, waging a brief, victorious war against the vast army of Gentile unbelievers led by the Satan indwelled Antichrist.

Following this armies defeat, Christ thrusts the Antichrist and the False Prophet temporally into Hell with all other unbelievers - where they are mocked unmercifully. They are later resurrected, receiving their eternal bodies, and assigned permanently into the Lake of Fire. The Devil is thrust into the Abyss where he and all his demons suffer in fire (they suffer separated from adjacent Hades, where non-believing humans reside). Both dwelling places are exceedingly uncomfortable, yet they are temporary holding locations, because inhabitants are eventually thrown into the permanent Lake of Fire.

The Tribulation period comes to an end. Jesus Christ has returned with the hosts of heaven as well as the Church and is ready to establish the 1000 Year Kingdom on earth.

A Brief, 75-day Post Tribulation Period

This 75-day period is neither part of Tribulation nor part of the following 1000 Year Kingdom (Kingdom). Instead, it bridges one to the other, and accommodates certain events that take place in preparation for the Kingdom.

The first 30 days are cleansing of the land and preparing it for the Kingdom. The next 45 days are for preparing those who may enter the Kingdom.

During the first 30-days a new and grand temple will be built for the opening of the Kingdom. Also, the earth and heavens will be renewed to make earth livable again.

During the following 45-days the Devil is chained and thrust into the abyss for 1000 years. OT Saints are resurrected into their new eternal bodies. All murdered Gentile Tribulation Saints who became believers during Tribulation are resurrected into their new eternal bodies.

The 144,000 Petra Jews, as well as every other remaining Jew still alive when Tribulation ends, will be believers and all will receive their resurrected, eternal bodies at the end of the Kingdom Period.

Five groups of believers thus enter the 1000 Year Kingdom Period... (a) resurrected Church Saints... (b) resurrected OT Saints... (c) resurrected Gentile Tribulation Saints (who have died after becoming believers during Tribulation) ... (d) Living, not resurrected Tribulation Jews who have not experienced earthly death and (e) living, believing, not resurrected Tribulation Gentiles who have not experienced earthly death. These still-alive Jews and Gentiles will enter the Kingdom Period with their earthly, natural bodies.

No unbelievers will enter the Kingdom Period! At the end of the 75-days following Tribulation, all preparations have been made for the Kingdom to start:

- The earth has been restored.
- The temple has been cleansed and rebuilt in a new and better way.
- The evil of the world has been set aside at least for a time.

1000 YEAR KINGDOM
FOLLOWS

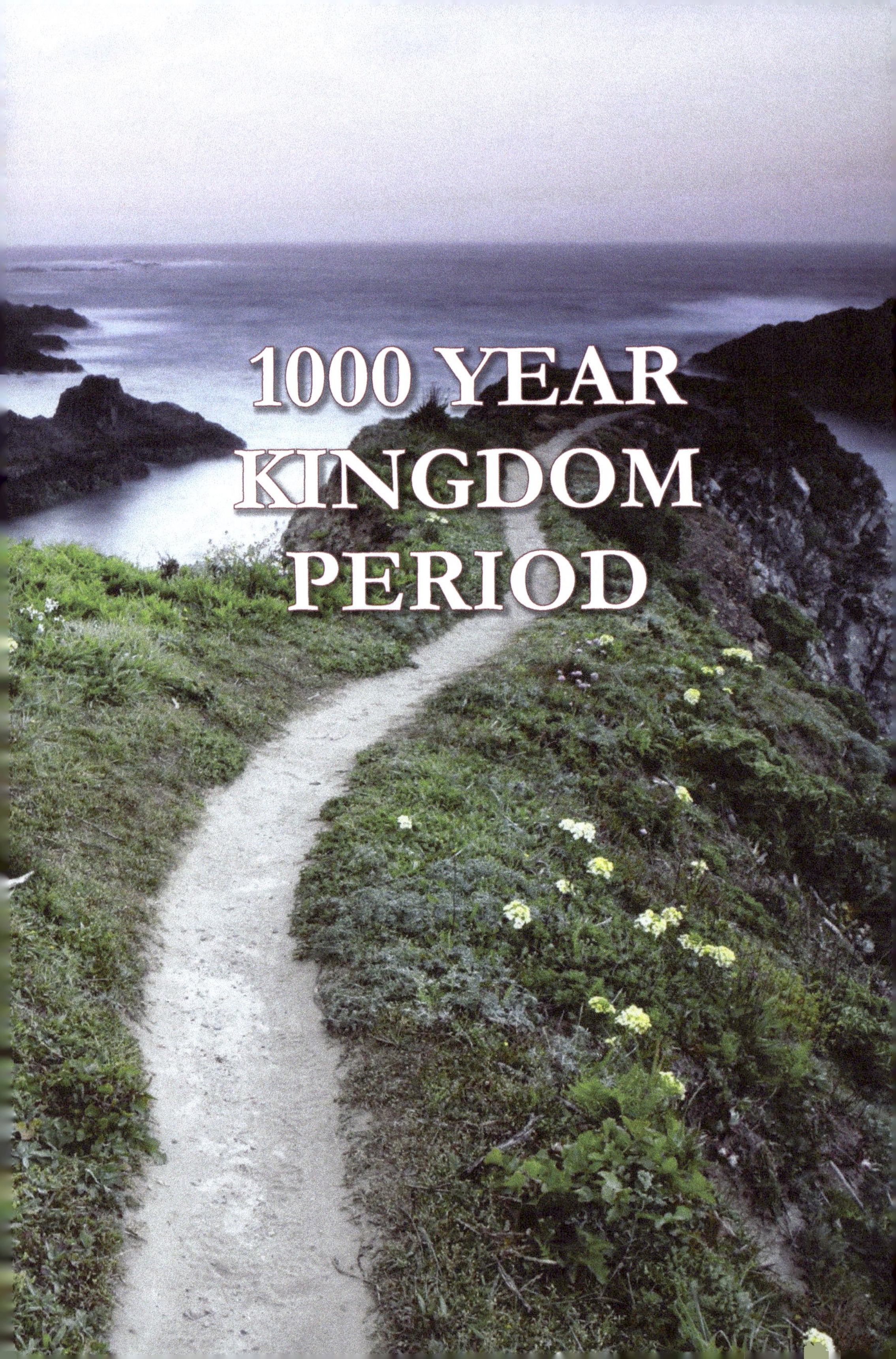
1000 YEAR
KINGDOM
PERIOD

1000 YEAR KINGDOM PERIOD

IN BRIEF: This 1000 year future period of time following Tribulation, is where Christ has returned to earth and is sovereign overall.

An overview:
- The earth will again be like Eden.
- Fresh water will be everywhere and food abundant.
- There will be animals, but absent their predator-prey relationship with men.
- Jesus will rule all the earth's nations from the Temple in Jerusalem.
- Daily life will be awesome for all people of all nations.

So, the Kingdom Period begins, following the Antichrist and False Prophet having been thrust into the eternal Lake of Fire and the Devil, chained, and consigned into the Abyss for 1000 years. The purpose of the Kingdom is to be a capstone on the earth's existence, highlighting Jesus' perfect rule.

During these 1000 years on earth, Christ reigns as the undisputed King ruling from Jerusalem with King David making a comeback as second in charge. There are numerous nations, but all are in service under Christ's governance. The government's center is Jerusalem.

This is a joyous 1000 years with Jesus being the perfect judge. There are biblical signs that all Kingdom Period people (Millennials) will prosper without many of today's modern conveniences and inventions. The Bible clearly states all Millennials will forget all about war and instruments of war. During 1000 years of peace, it's no wonder people no longer will remember what national conflict and war was like.

To repeat… five God chosen groups will inhabit the earth during this 1000 Year Kingdom Period. They are:
     (a) Resurrected Church Saints
     (b) Resurrected OT Saints
     (c) Resurrected Tribulation Saints (Jews and
        Gentiles who have died during Tribulation)
     (d) All, still alive, Tribulation Jews
     (e) All, still alive, believing Tribulation Gentiles

Having not experienced an earthly death and being believers, all humanly alive Jews and Gentiles enter the Kingdom Period with their earthly, non-resurrected, natural bodies.

In other words, they are normal living and breathing people just like you and I are today… but they are believers, secure in having been saved, followers of Christ.

Being natural people (still with sinful earthly bodies), they can and will commit sins and marry and have children.

Saints with resurrected bodies who will live alongside with them, will not marry nor have children.

As noted, these Millennial born sinful natured Jew and Gentile neighbors, who are also believers, will marry and have children. These children, as Scripture reminds us, are born with sinful natures. These children, and their future generations… may, or may not, become believers. Over time these Millennial-born people will repopulate the earth.

It is unclear (but expected) that during these 1000 years Christ will ensure that all Israelites and their future generations will become believers.

But for Gentiles it is clear that their future generations will include non-believers as well as believers.

So, sin will be present during this 1000 Year Kingdom Period, but all events will be under grace because Christ reigns over all the earth.

Birth, life, and death during the 1000 Year Kingdom Period will be different from today. There will no longer be child death in infancy, and every person born in the Kingdom will live at least 100 years.

The offspring of Gentiles born in the Kingdom who do not become believers by their 100th birthday will die at the age of 100, and their spirits will then enter Hades.

Only those with faith in Jesus will be allowed to live the full 1000 years.

All Millennial Saints will of course live through the end of the Millennial Kingdom.

New Millennial Saints (Jewish and Gentile believers) who are without eternal, sin free bodies receive resurrected bodies at the conclusion of the 1000 years.

In summary, during these 1000 years, Christ is the undisputed King ruling from Jerusalem with King David being second in charge under Christ.

Throughout the earth, this will be a joyous 1000 years with Jesus being the perfect judge.

There will be numerous Gentile nations during the Millennial, but all are in service under Christ's leadership. However, there will be many unbelievers populating the earth!

Satan spends the full 1000 years away from mankind, and unable to tempt anyone. Satan is the author of all false knowledge on earth, and He has always used his lies to trick the world concerning God and sin.

Another Brief Interval, This One After Kingdom Period:

As the 1000 Year Kingdom Period ends, there is a brief interval (some estimate 7 years) before "into eternity" begins. During this interval, Satan is released from his prison, and God allows Satan to begin deceiving the unbelievers in Gentile nations, teaching them how to wage war and tempting them to wage war against Christ and Israel.

An active Devil temps an evil man, Gog, from the land of Magog (Eastern Europe), to lead a war effort that will involve a vast number of non-believers from all the Gentile nations of the earth. Their goal is to conquer Israel.

Christ using fire from Heaven destroys the Devil's warring horde as they attack. This failed invasion against a defenseless Israel is how the Lord brings about Satan's end.

This brief war results in a vast number of enemy dead bodies and instruments of war, strewn everywhere. Cleansing of the land will take considerable time.

At this point the Devil is assigned to his everlasting home, the Lake of Fire – joining the Antichrist and False Prophet who are already there. Satan is thereafter tormented forever and ever. The Lord has intentionally delayed judgement for Satan until the end of the age.

The First Resurrection was for believers... the forthcoming Second Resurrection is for unbelievers.

With the Kingdom Period ended and the interval about over, all unbelievers have died. Just as the Kingdom Period did not start until all believers were ready to enter together... neither can the final judgment take place until all unbelievers are judged.

Each person (all believers and unbelievers) born since the creation of man at some point in time receives a resurrected body.

Those unbelievers who failed to trust in God for forgiveness of sin will receive their eternal bodies during the interval at the end of the Kingdom Period.

This is a final judgement that the Bible calls The Great White Throne Judgement.

It takes place after the Kingdom Period and after Satan is thrown into the Lake of Fire where the Antichrist and the False Prophet reside.

Heavenly books are opened where are recorded everyone's deeds, whether good or evil.

Also at this time, another book is opened, called the Book of Life.

It is this book that specifies whether a person will inherit eternal life with God or receive everlasting punishment in the Lake of Fire.

While believers are held accountable for their actions, they are forgiven in Christ and their names have been written in the Book of Life from the creation of the world.

Anyone's name that is not found written in the Book of Life will be thrown into the Lake of Fire.

This is the final judgement of unbelievers.

The interval following the Kingdom Period ends.

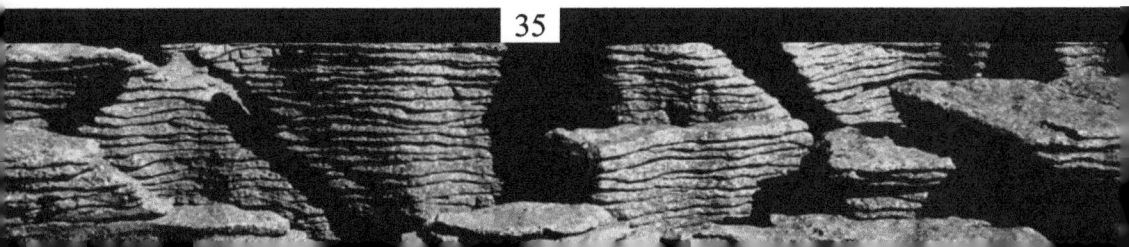

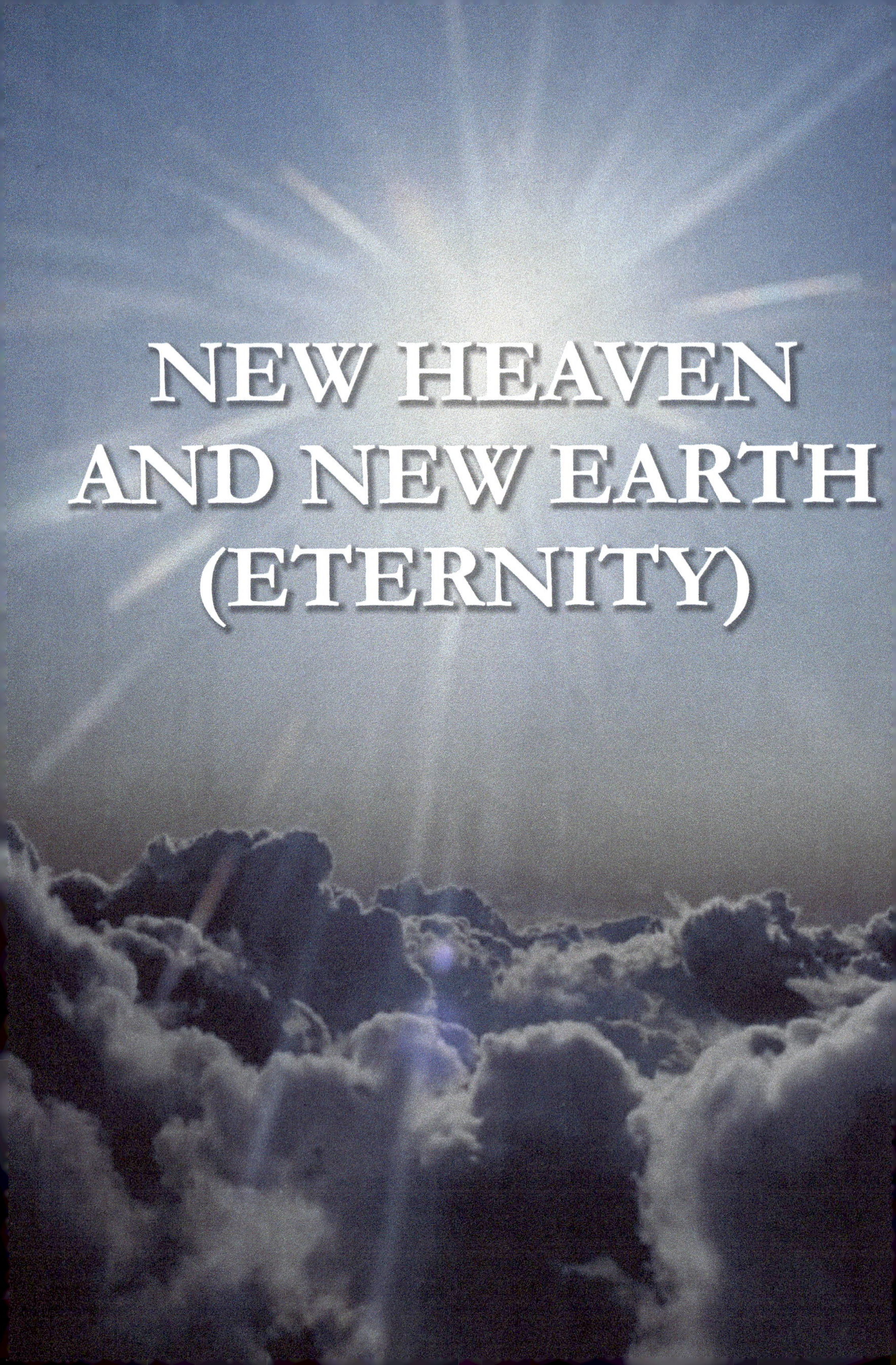

NEW HEAVEN AND NEW EARTH (ETERNITY)

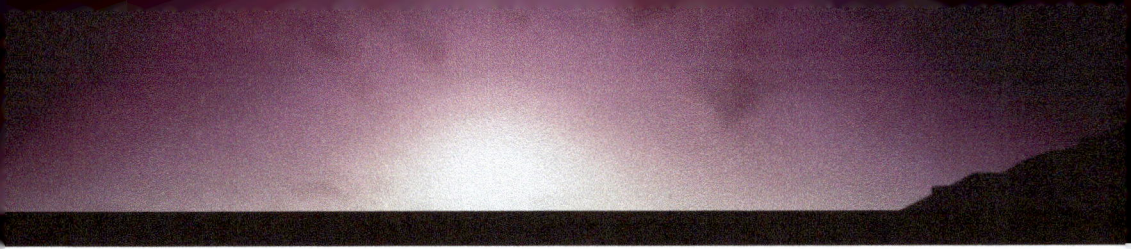

NEW HEAVEN AND NEW EARTH (ETERNITY)

IN BRIEF: Our current Heaven and earth will pass away, to be replaced by the new Heaven and the new earth.

Following the Kingdom Period, God's present creation of the earth and the entire planetary system will have been destroyed… to be found no more.

In its place, the Lord will make a new Heaven and new earth. This new creation completely replaces the old.

This new creation descends out of God's dwelling place in Heaven. This is an entirely new creation to replace the existing one.

Gentiles and Israel will be fellow heirs in the household of God. The dividing line wall between the two will exist no more.

There will be a city of Jerusalem and nations outside the city.

There will be a Tree of Life and we all will enjoy its fruit.

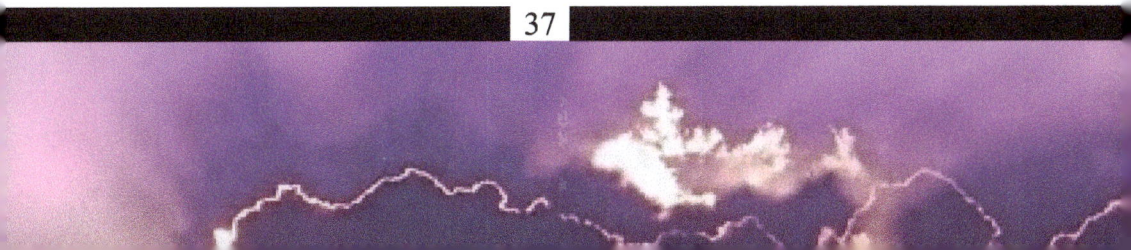

The work we do will be in service to Christ and while specifics aren't given, it's guaranteed our work will be enjoyable and fulfilling and important.

We will fully appreciate the love of God.

God the Father, and Christ and the Holy Spirit will reside alongside all saved humanity, in new imperishable, everlasting bodies, and we will live forever together.

AMEN

BIBLE REFERENCES

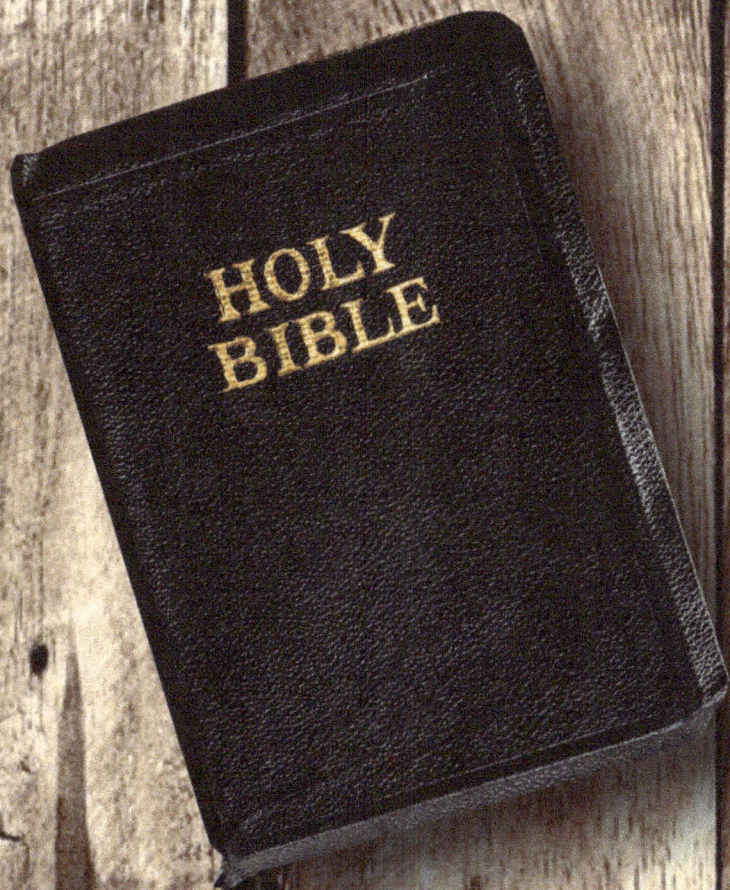

HOLY
BIBLE

Bible
References

Premillennial View
Bible Revealed "Future Events"

We believe that God's plan for humanity will follow an
orderly process, with a biblically revealed series of
"future events" including The Rapture, followed by
Tribulation, then Millennium or Kingdom Period, ending
with a New Heaven and New Earth.

NASB Bible Version Used Principally Throughout

***

There are other well documented views

God, Christ and Holy Spirit Are

Heaven and Earth Created
Man Created
Man Driven from Eden
Great Flood (Before 2500 BC)

God's Covenant with Abram (Abraham) (≈2081 BC)
Exodus: Jews Escape Egypt (≈1446 BC)
Jews Enter Holy Land (≈1406 BC)
N. Kingdom (10 Tribes) Falls to Assyria (≈722 BC)
S. Kingdom (2 Tribes) Falls to Babylonians (≈586 BC)
Christ's First Coming
Christ's Crucifixion and Resurrection
Pentecost
Church Age for Gentiles Begins

The Rapture

Tribulation...
Two Witnesses
The 144,000
War of Armageddon Begins
Christ's Second Coming
War of Armageddon Won

1,000-Year Kingdom
Christ Rules
War of Gog & Magog
Great White Throne Judgment

New Heaven and New Earth

OUR SPIRITS EXIST ETERNALLY:

Matthew 25:46 speaks of everlasting consciousness.

[46]"These will go away into eternal punishment, but the righteous into eternal life."

SIX DWELLING REALMS FOR SOULS:

There are many biblical references to the earth, Heaven, Hell, Abyss, and Lake of Fire. The abode "Abraham's Arms (or Bosom)" is found only once in the New Testament, in the story of the rich man and Lazarus. Luke 16: 19-31.

CHRIST DESCENDED TO ABRAHAM'S ARMS (or BOSOM):

Ephesians 4:8-10

[8] Therefore it says,

"When He ascended on high, He led captive the captives, And He gave gifts to people." [9] (Now this *expression*, "He ascended," what does it mean except that He also had descended into the lower parts of the earth? [10]He who descended is Himself also He who ascended far above all the heavens, so that He might fill all things.)

CHURCH AGE:

The Church Age is the period of time from Pentecost in Acts 2, to The Rapture, foretold in 1 Thessalonians 4:13-18. It is called the Church Age because it covers the period in which the Church is on earth.

THE RAPTURE

THE RAPTURE IS A TIME OF RESURRECTION:

All those who have placed their trust in Jesus Christ during the Church Age, and have died before Jesus returns, will be resurrected at the Rapture. The Church Age began on the Day of Pentecost and will end when Christ returns to take believers back to Heaven with Him.

The Apostle Paul explained that not all Christians will die, but all will be changed, (given resurrected bodies).
1 Corinthians 15: 50-53 [50]Now this I say, brethren, that flesh and blood cannot inherit the kingdom of God; nor does corruption inherit incorruption. [51]Behold, I tell you a mystery: We shall not all sleep, but we shall all be changed [52] in a moment, in the twinkling of an eye, at the last trumpet. For the trumpet will sound, and the dead will be raised incorruptible, and we shall be changed. [53] For this corruptible must put on incorruption, and this mortal must put on immortality.

TIMING OF RESURRECTIONS:

In Bible times the harvest was conducted in three stages. It began with the gathering of the first fruits which were offered in thanksgiving to God.

It continued with the general harvest. But some of the crop was left in the field to be gathered by the poor and the needy. This was called the gleaning Leviticus 19: 9-10.

Using this imagery, the Bible presents the resurrection of Jesus as the "first fruits" of the resurrection of the righteous.

The gathering of the Church Age Saints, living and dead, at the appearing of the Lord at the Rapture is the general harvest stage of the resurrection of the righteous John 14:1-3 **and** 1 Thessalonians 4:13-18.

There's a third stage to this resurrection of the righteous. It's the gleanings, and it occurs at the end of the Tribulation when the Lord's Second Coming takes place.

At that time two groups of the righteous will be resurrected: (a) the Tribulation Martyrs Revelation 20:4, and (b) the Old Testament Saints Dan 12:2. The book of Daniel confirms that the Old Testament Saints will be resurrected at the end of the *"time of distress"* Daniel 12:1-2.

Those who become believers during the Millennial are the last Saints to be resurrected.

Non-believers will also be resurrected at this time, but to suffer eternal punishment. See the Great White Throne Judgement Revelation 20: 11-14.

RAPTURE IS ALSO A TIME OF JUDGEMENT WHERE SAINTS RECEIVE REWARDS:

Believers will receive their eternal rewards at the judgment seat of Christ, which occurs in conjunction with their resurrection at the Rapture.

1 Thessalonians 4:16-17 [16]For the Lord Himself will descend from heaven with a shout, with the voice of the archangel and with the trumpet of God, and the dead in Christ will rise first. [17]Then we who are alive, who remain, will be caught up together with them in the clouds to meet the Lord in the air, and so we will always be with the Lord.

Luke 14:13-14 [13]But whenever you give a banquet, invite people who are poor, who have disabilities, who are limping, and people who are blind; [14]and you will be blessed, since they do not have the *means* to repay you; for you will be repaid at the resurrection of the righteous.

Rev 22:12 [12]"Behold, I am coming quickly, and My reward *is* with Me, to reward each one as his work deserves".

TRIBULATION

TRIBULATION FOLLOWS THE RAPTURE:

The Bible does not reveal the start date of The Tribulation. It's believed that Tribulation's logical start date is closely, if not immediately following the Rapture.

The Great Tribulation begins when Satan is cast from Heaven to earth, including his angels.
Revelation 12: 7-9 [7]And there was war in heaven, Michael and his angels waging war with the dragon.

The dragon and his angels waged war,[8] and they did not prevail, and there was no longer a place found for them in heaven. [9]And the great dragon was thrown down, the serpent of old who is called the devil and Satan, who deceives the whole world; he was thrown down to the earth, and his angels were thrown down with him.

Revelation's seven seals are one of a series of end-times judgments from God. The seals are described in Revelation 6:1–17 and 8:1–5.

This Commentary has summarized The Tribulation as "A time of unprecedented difficulty". But within this narrative there is no detailing of the catastrophes involved with God's seals, trumpets, and bowls.

WHY TRIBULATION IS NECESSARY

Tribulation is called a time of Israel's distress, and yet Jacob (i.e., the nation of Israel) will be saved from it. Therefore, the chief purpose of Tribulation is to bring Israel back to the Lord, referencing Ezekiel, Ezekiel 20 36-38 [36]Just as I entered into judgment with your fathers in the wilderness of the land of Egypt, so I will enter into judgment with you," declares the Lord God. [37]"I will make you pass under the rod, and I will bring you into the bond of the covenant; [38]and I will purge from you the rebels and those who revolt against Me; I will bring them out of the land where they reside, but they will not enter the land of Israel. So, you will know that I am the Lord.

TRIBULATION'S 7-YEAR PERIOD

The Jewish lunar calendar year has 360 days... Tribulation's seven-year period consists of two periods of 1260 days (2520 days in total).

An angel told Daniel that a week (shabbat) or 7-year period would end our current age.

- And the event that kicks off that 7-year period will be the signing of a covenant between the Antichrist and Israel.
- This covenant will allow the Jews to sacrifice in a newly constructed temple on the Temple Mount, but after 3 ½ years this covenant is broken.

Dan 9:27 [27] And he will confirm a covenant with the many for one week, but in the middle of the week he will put a stop to sacrifice and grain offering; and on the wing of abominations will come the one who makes desolate, until a complete destruction, one that is decreed, gushes forth on the one who makes desolate.

THE 144,000 TRIBULATION JEWS

Revelation 7:4 [4] And I heard the number of those who were sealed: 144,000, sealed from every tribe of the sons of Israel.

This verse identifies 144,000 Jewish men living during Tribulation, 12,000 taken from every tribe of the children of Israel.

Revelation 7:9 [9] After these things I looked, and behold, a great multitude which no one could count, from every nation and *all the* tribes, peoples, and languages, standing before the throne and before the Lamb, clothed in white robes, and palm branches *were* in their hands.

Through their testimony a great multitude that no one could count, from every nation, tribe and language will come to faith in Christ.

The 144,000 Jewish evangelists of The Tribulation will not be believers until after the Tribulation begins, for if they had been believers beforehand, then they would have been removed from the earth at the Rapture with those of the Church.

Only after the Spirit touches their hearts do these men become aware of their commission and purpose in the Tribulation.

THE 144,000 AND ALL BELIEVING JEWS, MOVED FOR PROTECTION TO PETRA:

Isaiah 33:14-16

[14]Sinners in Zion are terrified;
Trembling has seized the godless.
"Who among us can live with the consuming fire?
Who among us can live with everlasting burning?"
[15]One who walks righteously and speaks with integrity,
One who rejects unjust gain
And shakes his hands so that they hold no bribe;
One who stops his ears from hearing about bloodshed
And shuts his eyes from looking at evil;
[16]He will dwell on the heights,
His refuge will be the impregnable rock;
His bread will be given *him*,
His water will be sure.

Micah 2:12

12"I will certainly assemble all of you, Jacob,
I will certainly gather the remnant of Israel.
I will put them together like sheep in the fold;
Like a flock in the midst of its pasture
They will be noisy with people.

At the mid-point of Tribulation, the Lord moves to prepare the Earth for the next 3 ½ years. Among those moves is the establishment of a place of protection for all those believing Jews on earth which includes the 144,000 Jewish men. This place of protection, Petra or Botzrah, will be a fortress in the desert for the second half of Tribulation.

WAR OF ARMAGEDDON

Armageddon is not a single battle, but a series of engagements, culminating in Christ's return to earth for the second time.

Revelation 16:12–16 is the record of what will happen toward the end of the Tribulation, when an angel pours out the sixth bowl judgment on the earth. The word *Armageddon* makes its only appearance in the Bible in this passage:

12The sixth angel poured out his bowl on the great river, the Euphrates; and its water was dried up, so that the way would be prepared for the kings from the east. **13**And I saw coming out of the mouth of the dragon, and out of the mouth of the beast, and out of the mouth of the false prophet, three unclean spirits like frogs; **14** for they are spirits of demons, performing signs, which go out to the kings of the entire world, to gather them together for the war of the great day of God, the Almighty.

[15]("Behold, I am coming like a thief. Blessed is the one who stays awake and keeps his clothes, so that he will not walk about naked and people will not see his shame.")
[16]And they gathered them together to the place which in Hebrew is called Har-Magedon.

— *Har-Magedon (Armageddon)* ---

The Hebrew word Har-Magedon, or "Mount Megiddo", is the predicted location of the battle.

In Revelation 19:11–20, a final battle occurs at Christ's second coming as the conquering Christ defeats the forces of the Antichrist. This is a description of the Battle of Armageddon revealed in Revelation 16.

CHRIST'S SECOND RETURN TO EARTH

Petra (or Bozrah) is geographically a fortress of rock, which was the capital and central city of the kingdom of Edom. As described earlier, at the mid-point of Tribulation, God miraculously will transfer all believing Jews to Petra for their protection from the Antichrist's immediate control and subsequent army attacks.

The second coming is when Jesus returns to defeat the Antichrist, destroy evil, and establish His Millennial Kingdom. Tribulation is nearing its end, described in Revelation 19.

Isaiah describes a Tribulation end-time when all the Gentile nations' armies, ruled by the Antichrist, are about to be destroyed by the Lord at His Second Coming.

Isaiah 34:1-6 [1]Come near you nations. To hear; and listen, you peoples! Let the earth and all it contains hear, and the world and all that springs from it. [2]For the Lord's anger is against all the nations, and His wrath against all their armies. He has utterly destroyed them. He has turned them over to slaughter. [3]So their slain will be thrown out, and their corpses will give off their stench. And the mountains will be drenched with their blood. [4]And all the heavenly lights will wear away, and the sky will be rolled up like a scroll. All its lights will also wither away as a leaf withers from the vine, or as one withers from the fig tree. [5]For My sword has drunk its fill in heaven. Behold it shall descend for judgment upon Edom, and upon the people whom I have designated for destruction.[6]The sword of the Lord is filled with blood, It drips with fat, with the blood of lambs and goats, with the fat of the kidneys of rams. For the Lord has a sacrifice in Bozrah, and a great slaughter in the land of Edom.

Isaiah's descriptions indicate that the Lord will initially defend the encampment of His people in Petra and destroy all who attack it. This action happens in conjunction with the Lord's descending from Heaven, at the end of Tribulation.

Jesus' arrival at Botzrah is in the final stage of the War of Armageddon when the Lord begins destroying the armies of the Antichrist there in Edom. The Lord alone does the fighting, and the text makes no mention of any other person or entity fighting – just the Lord.

So, the Lord descends as described in Revelation 19 with support behind Him, and as He arrives in Petra, He begins destroying the forces of the Antichrist.

From Petra, the Lord approaches Jerusalem. Zechariah writes that Satan has been allowed to attack and partially subdue Jerusalem because it serves God's purpose in putting pressure on the Jewish Nation to make a "national confession of faith" that Jesus is the Messiah.

Zechariah 13:7-9

[7]"Awake, sword, against My Shepherd,
And against the Man, My Associate,"
Declares the Lord of armies.
"Strike the Shepherd and the sheep will be scattered;
And I will turn My hand against the little ones.
[8]And it will come about in all the land,"
Declares the Lord,
"That two parts in it will be cut off and perish;
But the third will be left in it.
[9]And I will bring the third part through the fire,
Refine them as silver is refined,
And test them as gold is tested.
They will call on My name,
And I will answer them;
I will say, 'They are My people,'
And they will say, 'The Lord is my God.'"

Finally, Israel as a nation makes a national confession of faith that Jesus is the Messiah.

The War of Armageddon comes to an end.

THE DESTINIES OF THE ANTICHRIST AND FALSE PROPHET

As Tribulation ends, the Antichrist and False Prophet are temporally sent into Hell, amongst all other unbelievers, where they are mocked unmercifully (Isaiah 14), and later resurrected into new, eternal bodies, then assigned permanently into the Lake of Fire.

THE POST TRIBULATION 75-DAY INTERVAL

Dan 12:11 **11**And from the time that the regular sacrifice is abolished, and the abomination of desolation is set up, there *will* be 1,290 days.

Here Daniel refers back to one of the three familiar Tribulation anchors. He mentions the moment the regular sacrifice is abolished, at the midpoint anchor of Tribulation. From that midpoint anchor until the end of Tribulation there will be 1,260 days (or 3½ years).

See that in this case Daniel reveals a different number of days to count from the midpoint anchor. Beginning at the midpoint of Tribulation, Daniel says to count 1,290 days until the abomination of desolation is ended. The abomination is that image of the Antichrist that the false prophet sets up in the temple and made the world worship. After Jesus returns, it remains standing for a while until it's taken down. And the time required to remove it is 30 days after Jesus' second coming (1,290 days after mid-Tribulation).

Dan 12:12 **12** Blessed is the one who is patient and attains to the 1,335 days!

In Dan v. 12, Daniel's timeline extends a step further. Daniel says that those who are "blessed of the Lord" will be those who wait and attain to 1,335 days. That's another 45 days after the abomination of desolation is removed from the temple. Who are these who are waiting and what are they attaining? These additional 45 days will be a period for identifying those who may enter the Kingdom and giving them eternal bodies. Those who are blessed are those who have been waiting for the resurrection and now that time has come. At the end of the 45 days, they will finally attain what they have waited for.

Who are these still waiting for resurrection? The Church Saints have already attained resurrection, so this passage is about other Saints. Principally two groups of Saints will still be awaiting resurrection at the end of Tribulation. Old Testament Saints have yet to be resurrected, and the souls of Tribulation Saints martyred and under the altar are without resurrected bodies.

So altogether, there will be a 75-day interval between the end of Tribulation and the start of the Kingdom. The first 30 days are to clean the temple from the abomination and probably to cleanse the entire world of the destruction. While the remaining 45 days will be a period for resurrecting and rewarding those blessed to enter the Kingdom.

Thus:

- There is a 75-day interval between the end of Tribulation and the start of the Kingdom.
- First 30 days… grand temple built, and the land is cleansed.

Following 45 days…:

- Satan is thrust into the abyss for 1000 years.
- Living tribulation Saints and all living Jews are resurrected into their new eternal bodies.
- No unbelievers will enter the Kingdom.

1000 YEAR KINGDOM PERIOD

SEQUENCE OF SAINTS RESURRECTIONS

Detailed in the Rapture section.

DAVID IS SECOND IN CHARGE

Micah 4:3 [3]And He will judge between many peoples. And render decisions for mighty, distant nations Then they will beat their swords into plowshares, and their spears into pruning hooks. Nation will not lift a sword against nation. And never again will they train for war.

Micah v.3 says in this 1,000-Year Kingdom, the Lord renders decisions between the nations including mighty distant nations. So, while sin will exist, it will have no material impact on life since it will be under Christ's perfect rule.

Isaiah 9:6-7 [6]For a Child will be born to us, a Son will be given to us. And the government will rest on His shoulders. And His name will be called Wonderful Counselor, Mighty God, Eternal Father, Prince of Peace. [7]There will be no end to the increase of *His* government or of peace. On the throne of David and over His kingdom, to establish it and to uphold it with justice and righteousness from then on and forevermore. The zeal of the Lord of armies will accomplish this.

The government sits on His shoulders, meaning Jesus presides over a bureaucracy. The world is a big geography, and there will be many to rule over, so Christ enlists others in His government.

So Israel's most famous king, none other than King David, will return to rule over them as their prince serving under the authority of Christ, the King.

Jeremiah 30:8-9 [8]'It shall come about on that day,' declares the Lord of armies, 'that I will break his yoke from their necks and will tear to pieces their restraints; and strangers will no longer make them their slaves. [9]But they shall serve the Lord their God and David their King, whom I will raise up for them.

Ezekiel 34:23-24 [23]"Then I will appoint over them one shepherd, My servant David, and he will feed them; he will feed them himself and be their shepherd. [24]And I, the Lord, will be their God, and My servant David will be prince among them; I the Lord have spoken.

David returns and is appointed to rule over the land of Israel in Christ's government.

THE EARTH WILL BE LIKE A PARADISE

The Millennium (Millennial Kingdom) is the 1000-year reign of Jesus after the tribulation and before the Great White Throne Judgment of the wicked. During the millennium, Jesus will reign as king over Israel and all the nations of the world (Isaiah 2:4; 42:1). The world will live in peace (Isaiah 11:6–9; 32:18), Satan will be bound (Revelation 20:1–3), and, at its beginning, everyone will worship God (Isaiah 2:2–3).

The purpose of the 1000-year reign is to fulfill various promises God made to the world. Jesus' 1000-year reign will be a time of promises kept.

HOW CAN THERE BE UNBELIEVERS IN THE KINGDOM?

On the opening day of the Millennial Kingdom, the world will consist of believers only, but these believers will exist in two forms: (a) resurrected human beings in eternal, sinless bodies and (b) natural-born human beings still in temporal, sinful bodies.

The resurrected human beings will be those who died or were Raptured prior to the start of the Kingdom. They receive new resurrected, sinless bodies prior to the start of the Kingdom, both Old Testament and New Testament Saints, and enter the Kingdom in that form. These resurrected beings will never sin again, but they are not the only ones to enter.

The Kingdom world will also be populated initially by natural-born human believers who lived through the Tribulation, and therefore will enter the Kingdom in sinful, earthly bodies like those all of us occupy now.

These sinful natured individuals are Christians, so they may enter the Kingdom, but they continue to live in the same way we do now. They will marry, have children, and their offspring will also have sinful natured, earthly bodies.

These believers who enter the Kingdom coming out of Tribulation are the "sheep" separated from the "goats" in (Matthew 24). Since these believers did not die prior to the start of the Kingdom, they were never resurrected into glorified bodies. Therefore, they enter into the Kingdom in the nature of Adam and are able to reproduce as we do today.

Their descendants give rise to a growing, unbelieving population in the Kingdom.

KINGDOM LIFE SPANS

Isaiah 65:20

[20] No longer will there be in it an infant *who lives only a few days*,
Or an old person who does not live out his days;
For the youth will die at the age of a hundred,
And the one who does not reach the age of a hundred will be *thought* accursed.

Isaiah's poetry employs couplets in this verse to describe the rules of death in the Kingdom. The first and third lines go together while the second and fourth lines go together.

Analysis: God controls the timing of death in the Kingdom:
  a. Isaiah says that no longer will there be an infant who lives only a few days.
  b. The earliest a child will die is at the age of 100, and that person will be considered a youth.
  c. Isaiah says that an old man will never fail to live out his days in the Kingdom, meaning he will not die of old age.
  d. The one who does not pass the 100th year will be understood to be accursed.

To be accursed means to fall under divine judgment, which indicates eternal judgment in Hell. We know that only unbelievers are under condemnation from God, so those accursed must refer to unbelievers in the Kingdom. These are the nonbelieving offspring of the Gentile believers born into the Kingdom in natural bodies. They will die at age 100 and enter Hell at that point.

So, the 100th birthday seems to be the watershed moment for all those born in the Kingdom. Only those who believe in Jesus as Lord will be allowed to live longer than 100 years. Once a person believes, they become immune to death because Isaiah says they will live until the end of the Kingdom.

Summary: The unbeliever will live 100 years while believers will live the entire 1000-year duration of the Kingdom.

Because the above NASB Bible verse in Isaiah includes the wording - *"And the one who does not reach the age of a hundred will be thought accursed"* - there may be questions on whether the nonbeliever dies at 100 years of age, or some time prior to their 100 years of age. The Orthodox Jewish Bible (OJB) translation seems to help clarify:

Orthodox Jewish Bible (OJB) Isaiah 65:20:
20 There shall be no more in there an infant of days, nor a zaken (old man) that hath not filled his days; for he that shall die a hundred years old will be regarded a na'ar; but the choteh (sinner), a hundred years old, will be accursed.

Therefore the unsaved die at 100 years of age, all saints live the full 1000 years.

POST KINGDOM INTERVAL

The earlier covered post Tribulation 75-day interval in some ways, presents a precedent for recognizing a post Kingdom interval.

The entire Kingdom Period is a fulfillment of the Abrahamic Covenant given to Israel.

Revelation 20 tells us that there will be events that happen after the 1000 years are completed. And yet these events must be appended to the Kingdom period because they take place prior to the next age starting.

For example, in Revelation 20: 7-10, [7] When the thousand years are completed, Satan will be released from his prison, [8] and will come out to deceive the nations which are at the four corners of the earth, Gog and Magog, to gather them together for the war; the number of them is like the sand of the seashore. [9] And they came up on the broad plain of the earth and surrounded the camp of the saints and the beloved city, and fire came down from heaven and devoured them. [10] And the devil who deceived them was thrown into the lake of fire and brimstone, where the beast and the false prophet are also; and they will be tormented day and night forever and ever.

It's very clear that v.7 begins with, "When the thousand years are completed, Satan will...".   So, by the time verses cover later events of v.7, the allotted time has already run out on the 1000 Year Kingdom.

Once Satan is released, he immediately begins to deceive humanity leading to a war on earth for the first time since the end of Tribulation. The war will involve countless numbers of people from all the Gentile nations of the earth.   Their target is Israel, and more specifically, the temple in Jerusalem.

Ezekiel chapters 33-38 are devoted to prophecies related to the Kingdom. Ezekiel tells the story of the final war that ends the Kingdom period, the war of Gog and Magog. This war clearly happens after, not during, the 1000 Year Kingdom Period.

The exact time-period of this "interval" is not made known in the Bible, but realizing the time required for the number of events described to occur, it's estimated that the interval will be about 7 years.

GOG AND MAGOG

Gog and Magog appear in Ezekiel 38-39 and in Revelation 20:7–8. Gog is a man of evil from the land of Magog in Eastern Europe.

GREAT WHITE THRONE

The Great White Throne judgment is described in Revelation 20:11-15 and is the final judgment prior to the lost being cast into the lake of fire. We know from Revelation 20:7-15 that this judgment will take place after the Millennium and after Satan is thrown into the Lake of Fire where the beast and the False Prophet are (Revelation 19:19-20; 20:7-10).

The books that are opened (Revelation 20:12) contain records of everyone's deeds, whether they are good or evil, because God knows everything that has ever been said, done, or even thought, and He will reward or punish each one accordingly (Psalm 28:4; 62:12; Romans 2:6; Revelation 2:23; 18:6; 22:12).

Also at this time, another book is opened, called the "Book of Life" (Revelation 20:12). It is this book that determines whether a person will inherit eternal life with God or receive everlasting punishment in the Lake of Fire.

Although Christians are held accountable for their actions, they are forgiven in Christ and their names were written in the "Book of Life" from the creation of the world" (Revelation 17:8). We also know from Scripture that it is at this judgment when the dead will be "judged according to what they had done" (Revelation 20:12) and that "anyone's name" that is not "found written in the Book of Life" will be "thrown into the Lake of Fire" (Revelation 20:15).

NEW HEAVEN AND NEW EARTH

God causes the Old Heaven and Earth to "pass away". He reveals a New Heaven, a New Earth, and a New Jerusalem where there is no sin or death.

Revelation 21:5 "[5]And He who sits on the throne said, "Behold, I am making all things new." And He said, "Write, for these words are faithful and true."

This is John's vision of God's revealed future:

Rev. 21:9-27 [9]Then one of the seven angels who had the seven bowls, full of the seven last plagues, came and spoke with me, saying, "Come here, I will show you the bride, the wife of the Lamb."

The New Jerusalem:

[10]And he carried me away in *the* Spirit to a great and high mountain, and showed me the holy city, Jerusalem, coming down out of heaven from God, [11]having the glory of God. Her brilliance was like a very valuable stone, like a stone of crystal-clear jasper. [12]It had a great and high wall, with twelve gates, and at the gates twelve angels; and names *were* written on *the gates*, which are the *names* of the twelve tribes of the sons of Israel. [13]*There were* three gates on the east, three gates on the north, three gates on the south, and three gates on the west. [14]And the wall of the city had twelve foundation stones, and on them were the twelve names of the twelve apostles of the Lamb. [15]The one who spoke with me had a gold measuring rod to measure the city, its gates, and its wall. [16]The city is laid out as a square, and its length is as great as the width; and he measured the city with the rod, twelve thousand stadia; its length, width, and height are equal. [17]And he measured its wall, 144 cubits, *by* human measurements, which are *also* angelic *measurements*. [18]The material of the wall was jasper; and the city was pure gold, like clear glass. [19]The foundation stones of the city wall were decorated with every kind of precious stone. The first foundation stone was jasper; the second, sapphire; the third, chalcedony; the fourth, emerald; [20]the fifth, sardonyx; the sixth, sardius; the seventh, chrysolite; the eighth, beryl; the ninth, topaz; the tenth, chrysoprase; the eleventh, jacinth; the twelfth, amethyst. [21]And the twelve gates were twelve pearls; each one of the gates was a single pearl. And the street of the city was pure gold, like transparent glass.

[22] I saw no temple in it, for the Lord God the Almighty and the Lamb are its temple. [23] And the city has no need of the sun or of the moon to shine on it, for the glory of God has illuminated it, and its lamp is the Lamb. [24] The nations will walk by its light, and the kings of the earth will bring their glory into it. [25] In the daytime (for there will be no night there) its gates will never be closed; [26] and they will bring the glory and the honor of the nations into it; [27] and nothing unclean, and no one who practices abomination and lying, shall ever come into it, but only those whose names are written in the Lamb's book of life.

AMEN

NOTES

NOTES

NOTES